SUPERSTARS OF WRESTLING

BECKY LYNCH

BY BENJAMIN PROUDFIT

HOT TOPICS

Gareth Stevens
PUBLISHING

Please visit our website, www.garethstevens.com. For a free color catalog of all our high-quality books, call toll free 1-800-542-2595 or fax 1-877-542-2596.

Library of Congress Cataloging-in-Publication Data

Names: Proudfit, Benjamin, author.
Title: Becky Lynch / Benjamin Proudfit.
Description: New York : Gareth Stevens Publishing, 2022. | Series: Superstars of wrestling | Includes index.
Identifiers: LCCN 2020032241 (print) | LCCN 2020032242 (ebook) | ISBN 9781538265871 (library binding) | ISBN 9781538265857 (paperback) | ISBN 9781538265864 (set) | ISBN 9781538265888 (ebook)
Subjects: LCSH: Lynch, Becky, 1987- --Juvenile literature. | World Wrestling Entertainment, Inc.--Biography--Juvenile literature. | Women wrestlers--Ireland--Biography.
Classification: LCC GV1196.L96 P76 2022 (print) | LCC GV1196.L96 (ebook) | DDC 796.812092 [B]--dc23
LC record available at https://lccn.loc.gov/2020032241
LC ebook record available at https://lccn.loc.gov/2020032242

First Edition

Published in 2022 by
Gareth Stevens Publishing
111 East 14th Street, Suite 349
New York, NY 10003

Copyright © 2022 Gareth Stevens Publishing

Designer: Michael Flynn
Editor: Kristen Nelson

Photo credits: Cover, pp. 1, 7, 19, 21 Etsuo Hara/Getty Images; p. 5 (Becky Lynch) Bryan Steffy/Getty Images; p. 5 (Finn Bálor) Sylvain Lefevre/Getty Images; p. 9 J. Merritt/Getty Images; p. 11 Bobby Bank/Getty Images; pp. 13, 29 Harry Murphy/Sportsfile/Getty Images; p. 15 https://en.wikipedia.org/wiki/Becky_Lynch#/media/File:Becky_Lynch_at_NXT_in_March_2015.jpg; p. 17 Christof Stache/AFP/Getty Images; p. 23 Mat Hayward/Getty Images; p. 25 Santiago Felipe/Getty Images; p. 27 Kevin Mazur/Getty Images.

All rights reserved. No part of this book may be reproduced in any form without permission in writing from the publisher, except by a reviewer.

Printed in the United States of America

CPSIA compliance information: Batch #CSGS22: For further information contact Gareth Stevens, New York, New York at 1-800-542-2595.

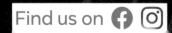

CONTENTS

A Young Wrestler 4

Career Setbacks 10

A New Start 12

Finding Her Way 16

Fan Favorite 20

WrestleMania Win 24

The Best of Becky Lynch 30

For More Information 31

Glossary 32

Index 32

A YOUNG WRESTLER

Becky Lynch was born Rebecca Quin on January 30, 1987, in Ireland. She loved **professional** wrestling from an early age. She was only 15 when she and her brother began training at a wrestling school in 2002.

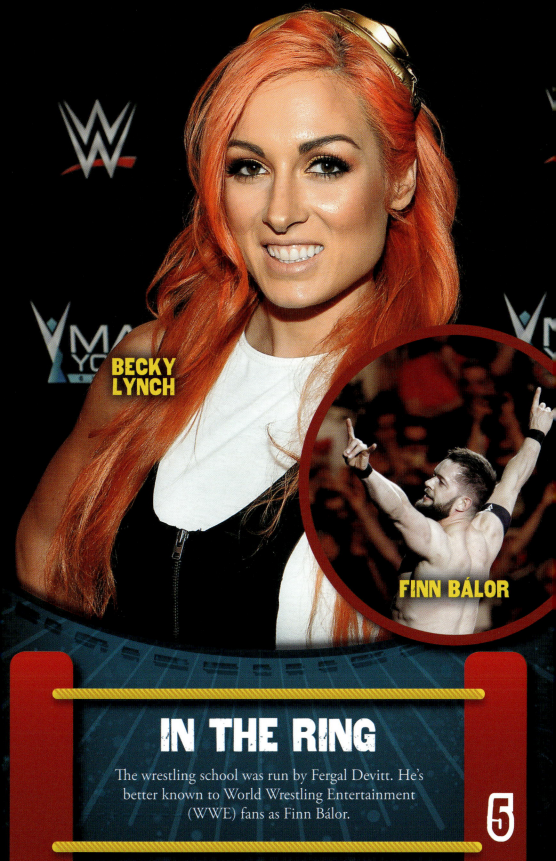

IN THE RING

The wrestling school was run by Fergal Devitt. He's better known to World Wrestling Entertainment (WWE) fans as Finn Bálor.

Even though the wrestling school was new and didn't have a ring at the start, Becky loved training there. She was in her first **match** in 2002. Her first one-on-one match was in February 2004. She was only 17!

IN THE RING

Becky's first ring name was Rebecca Knox.

Becky wrestled in England, Ireland, and other places in Europe. But women's wrestling was growing in North America. At 18, she got a Canadian **visa**. She started wrestling in Canada and the United States. In 2005, she took part in her first **tour** in Japan!

IN THE RING

At the time, Becky's dream was wrestling in the WWE.

CAREER SETBACKS

In May 2006, Becky wrestled for women's wrestling company SHIMMER. She was starting to make a name for herself. However, then her visa **expired**, and that fall, she got a **concussion** during a match. Becky didn't know if she'd wrestle again.

IN THE RING

After she got hurt, Becky worked as a flight attendant. She went back to school and also trained in gymnastics and martial arts.

A NEW START

In 2011, Becky spent time at SHIMMER as a manager. Soon after, she saw Fergal. He told her to wrestle again. She got in the ring while preparing to work on a TV show. It led her to try out for WWE company NXT.

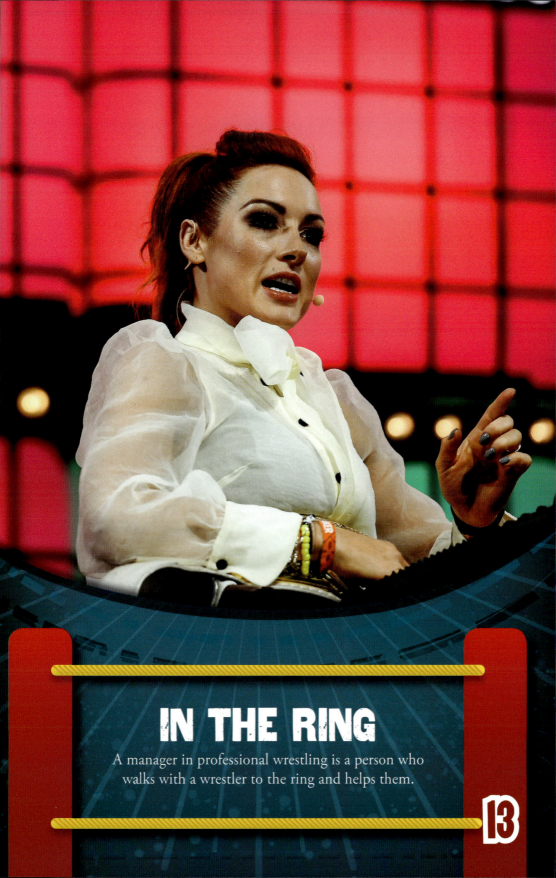

IN THE RING

A manager in professional wrestling is a person who walks with a wrestler to the ring and helps them.

Becky signed with NXT in April 2013. She had to work hard to get back in wrestling shape. But by the end of that year, she was performing on live shows. Becky made her NXT TV **debut** in May 2014.

IN THE RING

Lynch told ESPN: "When I first came over to WWE, I mean, just so full of hopes and dreams ... I had to build myself up again from scratch."

15

FINDING HER WAY

Becky was part of a group of women in NXT that called themselves the Four Horsewomen. They were Becky, Sasha Banks, Bayley, and Charlotte Flair. Together they made waves in professional wrestling. But Becky never won the NXT Women's Championship.

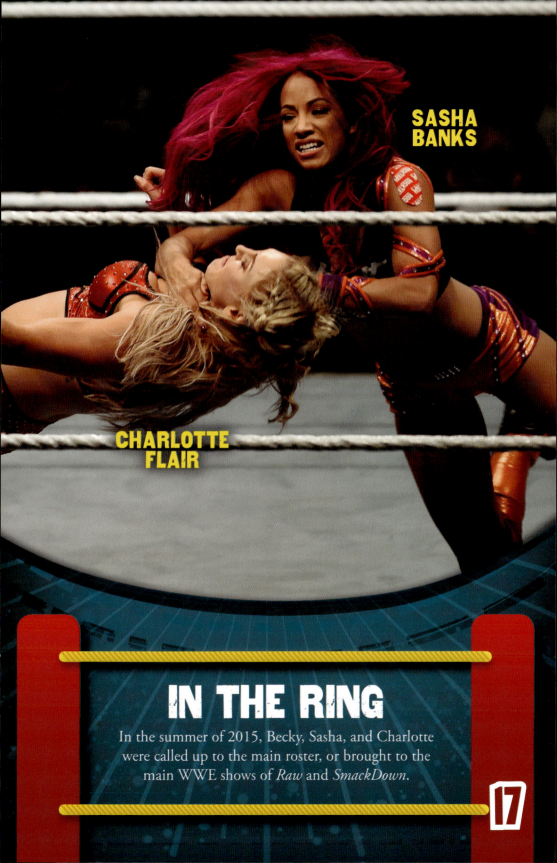

SASHA BANKS

CHARLOTTE FLAIR

IN THE RING

In the summer of 2015, Becky, Sasha, and Charlotte were called up to the main roster, or brought to the main WWE shows of *Raw* and *SmackDown*.

At first, Becky was part of Team PCB with Charlotte Flair and WWE superstar Paige. She became popular with fans, but still wasn't getting many championship chances. In 2016, Becky's first WrestleMania match was against Charlotte and Sasha Banks. Becky didn't win.

IN THE RING

Finally, Becky won the SmackDown Women's Championship in September 2016—but she didn't hold it for long.

FAN FAVORITE

By 2018, Becky's fans were getting louder. Then, she almost won the Women's Money in the Bank briefcase. At SummerSlam, Lynch lost to Charlotte Flair—again. So, she turned on Charlotte by slapping her and throwing her out of the ring. The crowd loved it!

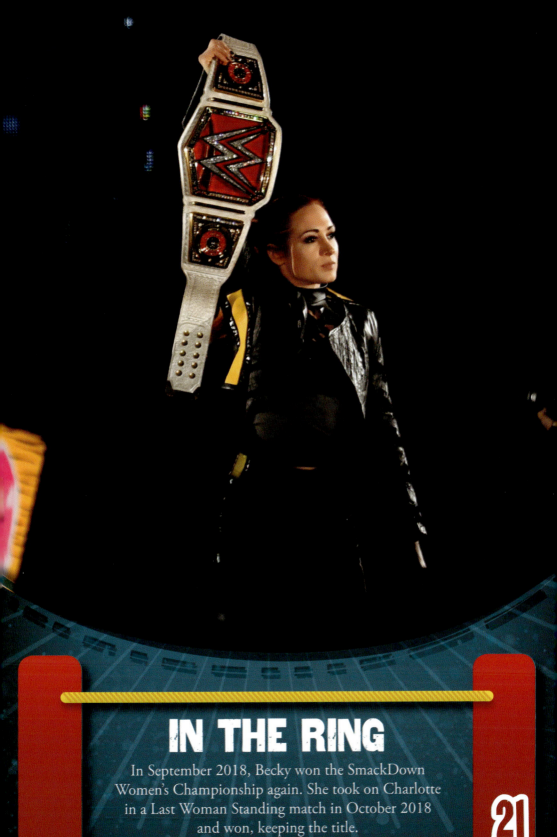

IN THE RING

In September 2018, Becky won the SmackDown Women's Championship again. She took on Charlotte in a Last Woman Standing match in October 2018 and won, keeping the title.

21

Becky—or "The Man"—was one of the most popular wrestlers in WWE as 2019 began. She entered the Women's Royal Rumble as one of the favorites to win. She did, sending Charlotte over the top rope! She earned a match at WrestleMania 35.

IN THE RING

"It is the biggest night of my life," she said about winning the Women's Royal Rumble.

WRESTLEMANIA WIN

Becky stepped into the WrestleMania 35 ring on April 7, 2019. She faced Ronda Rousey and Charlotte Flair in a triple threat match for both the Raw and SmackDown Women's Championships. She pinned Rousey, becoming the first person to ever hold both those titles!

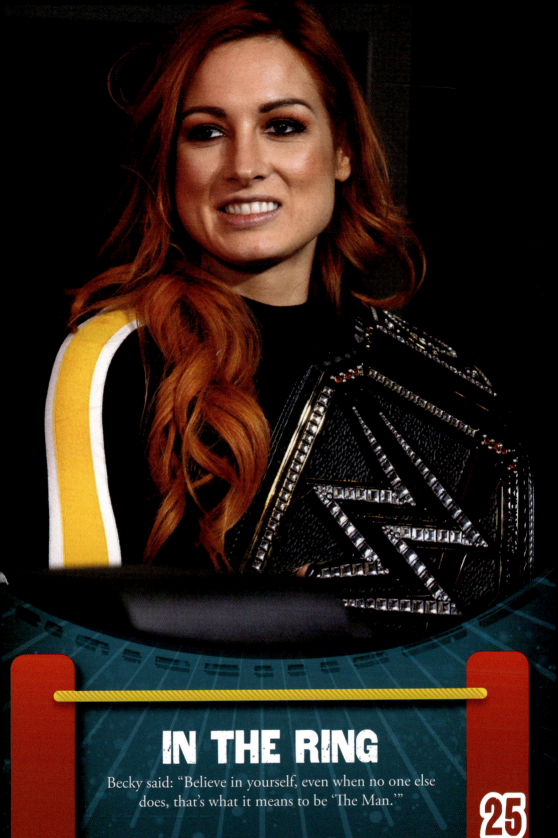

IN THE RING

Becky said: "Believe in yourself, even when no one else does, that's what it means to be 'The Man.'"

25

Becky lost the SmackDown Women's Championship to Charlotte at Money in the Bank. But by the end of 2019, Becky had become the longest-ever Raw Women's Champion. In January 2020, she beat Asuka at the Royal Rumble and kept the title.

IN THE RING

Becky got engaged to WWE superstar Seth Rollins in 2019.

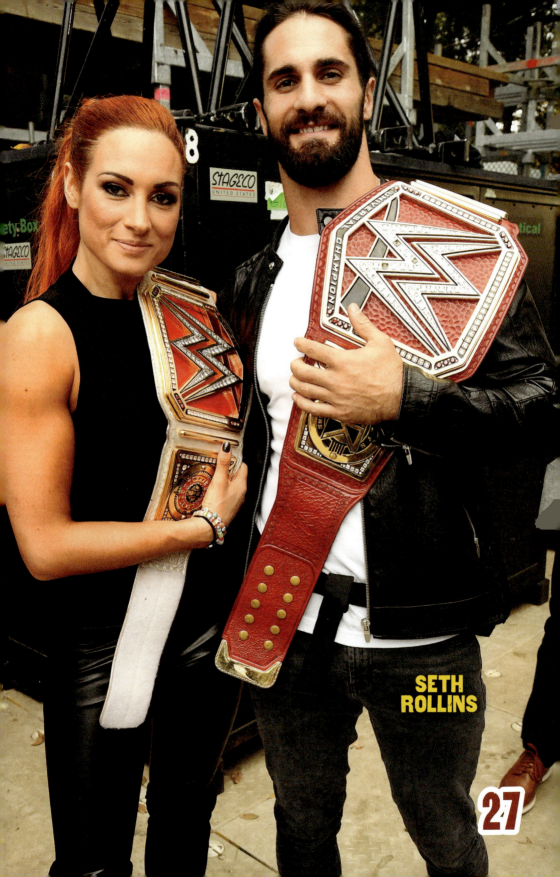

In May 2020, Becky announced she would take a break from wrestling to have a baby. Becky gave up the Raw Women's Championship to Asuka, ending her 399-day reign as champion. When will the Man return?

IN THE RING

Becky faced Shayna Baszler at WrestleMania 36 in April 2020. She won, keeping the Raw Women's Championship title.

THE BEST OF BECKY LYNCH

SIGNATURE MOVES
armbar, diving leg drop, hammerlock inverted DDT

FINISHERS
dis-arm-her, manhandle slam

ACCOMPLISHMENTS
SmackDown Women's Champion
2019 Women's Royal Rumble Winner
Longest-ever Raw Women's Champion
Part of first women's WrestleMania main event

MATCHES TO WATCH
2015 NXT TakeOver Unstoppable vs. Sasha Banks; 2018 Last Woman Standing Match vs. Charlotte Flair; 2019 Royal Rumble

FOR MORE INFORMATION

BOOKS

Abdo, Kenny. *Seth Rollins: The Architect*. Minneapolis, MN: Fly! An imprint of Abdo Zoom, 2020.

Pantaleo, Steve. *Ronda Rousey*. London, England: Dorling Kindersley, 2020.

WEBSITES

Becky Lynch—WWE
www.wwe.com/superstars/becky-lynch
Keep up to date on Becky's career with her official superstar profile.

WWE News, Video—ESPN
www.espn.com/wwe/
Check out ESPN's coverage of the WWE here!

Publisher's note to educators and parents: Our editors have carefully reviewed these websites to ensure that they are suitable for students. Many websites change frequently, however, and we cannot guarantee that a site's future contents will continue to meet our high standards of quality and educational value. Be advised that students should be closely supervised whenever they access the internet.

GLOSSARY

concussion: an injury to the brain caused by hitting the head very hard

debut: a first appearance

expire: to no longer be able to be used

match: a contest between two or more people

professional: earning money from an activity that many people do for fun

tour: a trip to many places in order to perform for people

visa: an official stamp that allows someone from another country to live elsewhere for a reason

INDEX

Asuka 26, 28
Banks, Sasha 16, 17, 18
Bayley 16
championships 16, 18, 21, 24, 26, 28
Devitt, Fergal 5, 12
Flair, Charlotte 16, 17, 18, 20, 21, 22, 24, 26
Four Horsewomen 16
NXT 12, 14, 16
Paige 18
Rollins, Seth 26, 27
Rousey, Ronda 24
SHIMMER 10, 12
Women's Royal Rumble 22, 23, 26
World Wrestling Entertainment (WWE) 5, 8, 12, 15, 17, 22
WrestleMania 18, 22, 24, 28